JUNIATA COLLEGE LIBRARY
CURRICULUM LIBRARY

P9-CLE-276

Artist BIOGRAPHIES

Georgia O'Keeffe

The Life of an Artist

Ray Spangenburg

Kit Moser

Enslow Publishers, Inc.

40 Industrial Road   PO Box 38
Box 398   Aldershot
Berkeley Heights, NJ 07922   Hants GU12 6BP
USA   UK

http://www.enslow.com

Georgia O'Keeffe

Copyright © 2002 by Enslow Publishers, Inc.

All rights reserved.

No part of this book may be reproduced by any means without the written permission of the publisher.

Library of Congress Cataloging-in-Publication Data

Spangenburg, Ray, 1939-
    Georgia O'Keeffe : the life of an artist / Ray Spangenburg and Kit Moser.
        p. cm. — (Artist biographies)
    Includes index.
    Summary: Presents the life of the twentieth-century American painter who drew much of her artistic inspiration from nature.
    ISBN 0-7660-1882-2
    1. O'Keeffe, Georgia, 1887-1986—Juvenile literature. 2. Artists—United States—Biography—Juvenile literature. [1. O'Keeffe, Georgia, 1887-1986. 2. Artists. 3. Painting, American. 4. Women—Biography.] I. Moser, Diane, 1944- II. Title. III. Artist biographies (Berkeley Heights, N.J.)
    N6537.O39 S68 2002
    759.13—dc21
                                          2002011985

Printed in the United States of America

10 9 8 7 6 5 4 3 2 1

To Our Readers: We have done our best to make sure all Internet addresses in this book were active and appropriate when we went to press. However, the author and the publisher have no control over and assume no liability for the material available on those Internet sites or on other Web sites they may link to. Any comments or suggestions can be sent by e-mail to comments@enslow.com or to the address on the back cover.

Illustration Credits: *American Artists in Photographic Portraits,* Dover Publications, Inc., 1995, p. 13; Art Resource, NY, pp. 26, 36; Chatham Hall, p. 10; Georgia O'Keeffe Museum, Santa Fe, New Mexico, p. 40; Library of Congress, p. 21; Malcolm Varon © 1987, p. 2; *New York Then and Now,* Dover Publications, Inc., 1976, p. 27; The Newark Museum/Art Resource, NY, pp. 23, 25, 32; Panhandle-Plains Historical Museum, p. 7; Smithsonian American Art Museum, Washington, DC/Art Resource, NY, pp. 5, 28; Todd Webb courtesy Evans Gallery, Portland, Maine, pp. 31, 35.

Cover Illustration: Malcolm Varon © 1987

Contents

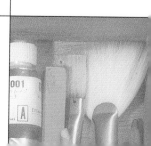

"I'm Going to Be an Artist"

When Georgia O'Keeffe first began painting in the early 1900s, people thought fine art could only be created by men. Only a few, very exceptional women had the chance to become serious artists. Women were not even allowed to vote in the United States back then. It was a man's world. But O'Keeffe did not let that stop her.

O'Keeffe's paintings were not always pictures of objects or people. She used shapes

Only One (1959). When O'Keeffe went up in an airplane, she was amazed at how rivers looked from high up in the sky. Many of her 1959 paintings, including this one, were inspired by that view.

and form and color to paint ideas and feelings. She was part of a new group of artists called modernists. Some people thought the new art was exciting. Other people thought it was silly. O'Keeffe didn't care. She knew what she wanted to paint. She did it and she did it well. Today, people all over the world still get a special feeling from her paintings.

Georgia Totto O'Keeffe was born November 15, 1887. She began life on a dairy farm near Sun Prairie, Wisconsin. People from many different parts of the world came there to find a better life. Georgia's grandparents were among them.

Georgia's father, Frank O'Keeffe, a handsome Irish-American, was a successful farmer and feed-store owner. His family had left Ireland to escape the potato famine of 1845–1850. They hoped to find better luck farming on the plains of Wisconsin.

Georgia's mother was Ida Totto, the daughter of a Hungarian count. Her father, George Totto, had left his home to escape war.

The Tottos and the O'Keeffes became neighbors in Wisconsin. Both families worked hard, and their farms did well. Frank and Ida grew up near each other. Both loved the land. When they married, they began their family on the Totto farm. They had seven children.

Georgia started out her life on a farm in Wisconsin. As a teenager, she moved with her family to a house in Virginia, where her family did not fit in well.

7

Georgia was the second child and the oldest girl among the seven. She grew up feeling that she was in charge of the younger children. She worked hard on the farm. Farm girls usually helped with washing, ironing, and baking. They also had chores to do outdoors. After chores were done, Georgia spent a lot of time alone. She liked the outdoors. The big hay barn across the fields became a symbol of her childhood.

Georgia always felt she was different from other children. "From the time I was small," she later recalled, "I was always doing things other people don't do."

Georgia had made up her mind in the eighth grade. When a school friend asked her what she planned to do when she grew up, she responded boldly. "I'm going to be an artist," she said.

In Sun Prairie, the O'Keeffe children attended a small school. Ida O'Keeffe wanted a better education for her children. So, in 1901, Georgia went to the Sacred Heart Academy in the nearby city of Madison. There, she received formal art classes for the first time.

In 1902, Georgia's family made a big change. The winters in Wisconsin were cold and windy. Frank O'Keeffe thought warmer winters would be better for his family's health. He sold the farm and moved his family to Williamsburg, Virginia.

Georgia and her brother Francis stayed behind in Wisconsin and lived with an aunt. They went to the big public high school in the city.

One day, Georgia's art teacher brought a jack-in-the-pulpit flower to class. She showed the students the parts of the flower. She pointed out its deep colors. It was the first time Georgia thought about drawing or painting plants. Many years later, she would become famous for her paintings of plants and flowers.

When Georgia joined her family the following year, Virginia was a shock to her. In Wisconsin, women and men had worked together to keep a farm going. Now, she lived in the South. Women

The seven other girls in Georgia's class at Chatham dressed like Southern belles. They wore their hair in ringlets. Georgia dressed in plain clothes and wore her hair in a ponytail.

had a different role. Having nice dresses, good manners, and a soft voice were more important.

Georgia finished high school at the Chatham Episcopal Institute, a boarding school for girls. She lived at the school in Chatham, Virginia. She kept on wearing the sensible clothes she was used to. She didn't let the other girls talk her into frills and ruffles. She thought the other girls were silly. They thought she was awkward and out of place. But they soon found she was also charming and a good friend. Georgia was the only art major to graduate in the class of 1905.

On graduation day, Georgia told her classmates, "I am going to live a different life from you girls. I am going to give up everything for my art."

Chapter 2

Finding the Artist Inside

O'Keeffe spent the next few years studying and searching. She was looking for the artist inside herself. In the fall of 1905, she went to study at the Art Institute of Chicago. Her studies there were interrupted when she got typhoid fever. Two years later, she attended the Art Students League in New York City.

O'Keeffe knew that New York was an important center for art. There, she studied under the famous artist William Merritt Chase.

William Merritt Chase was a successful painter of rich people's portraits. Georgia learned a lot from him. She began by copying his work.

He told his students not to get stuck doing only one type of art. "Take the best from everything," he said.

O'Keeffe did well in class. She received a scholarship for her work. Yet, her classmates did not take her seriously. After all, she was a woman, and most of them were men. They thought she was not a serious artist. One young man said to her, "I am going to be a great painter, and you will probably end up teaching painting in some girls' school."

One day, O'Keeffe went with a group of students to visit an art gallery. Some of the latest art from Europe was on exhibit—drawings by the French artist Auguste Rodin. The exhibit hall was called the 291 gallery because it was on the top floor of the building at 291 Fifth Avenue.

The man who owned the gallery was a famous photographer named Alfred Stieglitz. He was also the leader of a group of modernist artists. He and his friends had a lot of influence on art in New York. O'Keeffe watched Stieglitz talk. She thought he was loud and pushy. She was not excited about him or about modernism.

O'Keeffe was not happy with her studies, either. Chase taught his students to copy the great artists of the past. But this was not the art O'Keeffe felt deep inside. She longed to be considered good—even great. But she knew that art, to her, was not a matter of copying old works.

She decided to stop painting. For several years, even the smell of paint and turpentine made her sick!

O'Keeffe went to work drawing fashion advertisements. She drew lace and embroidery as a commercial artist. It was hard work, and she was under a lot of pressure. She was afraid of losing the special feeling she had about art. Then, she got the measles. Her eyes were so hurt by it that she couldn't continue the work.

In the spring of 1911, she began teaching art at her old school, Chatham Institute, in Virginia. O'Keeffe was a good, lively teacher. She found she liked the job. She also began to think about painting again.

Soon, she was taking art classes at the University of Virginia. She took classes from Alon Bement, a student of an artist named Arthur Wesley Dow. They both taught that art's purpose is to show a thought or feeling. Also, all the parts of a painting must work together. They must play in harmony, like instruments in a band.

Dow liked the Japanese idea of filling space with beauty. He said an artist needs to develop a sense of beauty. But this sense has to come from inside the artist. O'Keeffe liked this way of looking at art. It meant she had to feel every part of her life—and then put it on canvas.

That fall, O'Keeffe accepted a teaching job in the Amarillo, Texas, school system. It was her first introduction to the American West. She loved the big skies of Texas and the open desert lands.

"It had always seemed to me that the West must be wonderful," O'Keeffe later explained. She liked the openness and the beauty of the dry landscape. She thought it was a wonderful, wild world. For the next two years, she taught in her beloved Texas during the school year and at the University of Virginia during the summer.

During these years, O'Keeffe was soaking up experiences. She continued teaching summer school in Virginia. She took classes from Dow at Teachers College at Columbia University in New York. She taught at a women's college in South Carolina.

She also began work on a special series of drawings. She used charcoal and made curved lines and shaded areas. The drawings were simple but powerful. She was pleased with them. She knew they had come from deep within herself. She bundled them up and sent them to Anita Pollitzer, a friend in New York.

When Anita opened the package of drawings, she was excited. She put them under her arm and marched into the 291 gallery. Alfred Stieglitz was there. She showed him the drawings. He looked at them all. "At last," he said. "A woman's feelings on paper." Stieglitz had never really met Georgia. Yet, he felt he could see who she was from her drawings.

Stieglitz and O'Keeffe began writing letters to each other. Georgia was thrilled that Stieglitz understood what she was trying to express with her drawings.

Chapter 3

O'Keeffe and Stieglitz

The following July, something both wonderful and terrible happened. Alfred Stieglitz hung Georgia O'Keeffe's twelve drawings on the walls of the 291 gallery. There was just one problem with that. He had not asked her permission first. He had not even told her!

O'Keeffe was in New York that summer for classes at Columbia Teachers College. She was very angry when she found out what Stieglitz had done. He should have asked her first. She went to the gallery to make him take the drawings down.

They were too beautiful to take down, Stieglitz argued. He said that she could not keep her "children" to herself.

Finally, she left the drawings hanging on the walls of 291. Stieglitz won.

That fall, O'Keeffe went back to Texas. This time she was head of the art department at West Texas State Normal College in Canyon. O'Keeffe loved the canyons and desert hills in this region of the state. The Palo Duro Canyon was like the Grand Canyon but much smaller. She hiked and camped there. She began painting again.

In 1917, Stieglitz gave O'Keeffe a solo exhibit at the 291 gallery.

Alfred Stieglitz liked O'Keeffe's drawings. He thought they were strong and original. In 1916, he showed her drawings at his 291 gallery.

It was an exciting triumph for her. That same year, O'Keeffe made her first trip to New Mexico. She was stunned by the beauty of the place. She had never seen such wonderful light, not even in Texas.

The following year, O'Keeffe left Texas and teaching for good. From then on, she would devote her life to her artwork. She moved to New York and spent most of her time painting and drawing.

In 1924, she and Stieglitz married. He was twenty-three years older than she was, but they thought alike about many things. They also had a lot of respect for each other. She enjoyed his praise and encouragement. He loved her lively ways and bright mind. He also admired her beauty and loved to photograph her.

From the early 1920s until 1929, O'Keeffe spent every summer at Lake George, New York, with

Green Leaves (1923). O'Keeffe spent a lot of time in Lake George, New York. It is a region of mountain forests that are lush and green. She wrote in a letter to a friend that she felt "smothered with green."

Stieglitz's family. The lake was beautiful. The water was clear and cold. Pine forests along the shore provided shade. The buildings at the Stieglitz summer home were country barns and sheds that reminded O'Keeffe of her childhood in Wisconsin. She planted a garden. She painted the trees and the lake. She painted the barns.

She was happy to have the freedom to paint.

Chapter 4

Giant Blossoms and City Scenes

Sometime in 1924, O'Keeffe began painting flowers. O'Keeffe's flower paintings were different from most, though. Her flowers were not small and dainty. They were not pale and gentle like the flowers of other artists. She made her flowers huge and awesome. She made them bright and bold. No one had ever painted flowers this way before. People were amazed.

A year after they were married, O'Keeffe and Stieglitz moved to the thirtieth floor of the

Purple Petunias (1925). In 1924 O'Keeffe began her flower phase. She painted petunias, calla lilies, and zinnias. She painted them larger than life. The style was all her own.

Autumn Leaves No. 2 (1927). O'Keeffe did many paintings of clusters of leaves or of just one leaf at a time. In some of the paintings, the leaves are quite abstract. In other words, they may not look exactly like real leaves. Instead, you get a strong sense of their shapes and colors and the artist's feelings about leaves.

Shelton Hotel in New York. The view of the city from that height was thrilling. O'Keeffe had never lived so high up before.

In the 1920s, some art critics did not like the new buildings in New York. They liked the grace of the cathedrals of Europe. They liked castles on hilltops. The new buildings, they said, looked like "boxes with holes in them." They thought artists should paint country scenes. Woods, rolling grasslands, and

O'Keeffe was one of the first artists to paint the new skyscrapers in New York. These tall buildings were changing the shape of the city.

Painting Flowers

Years later, O'Keeffe explained, "Nobody sees a flower, really, it is so small. We haven't time—and to see takes time, like to have a friend takes time."

"If I could paint the flower exactly as I see it no one would see what I see because I would paint it small like the flower is small. So I said to myself— I'll paint what I see— what the flower is to me, but I'll paint it big, and they will be surprised into taking time to look at it—I will make even busy New Yorkers take time to see what I see of flowers." She was right. Everyone noticed.

Yellow Calla (1926).

fields of flowers seemed more worthy of being painted than city streets, tall buildings, traffic, and factories.

O'Keeffe did not agree. She decided to try to paint New York. Later, she wrote, "Of course, I was told that it was an impossible idea—even the men hadn't done too well with it. From my teens on, I had been told that I had crazy notions, so I was accustomed to disagreement and went on with my idea of painting New York." She completed her first painting of the city in 1925.

O'Keeffe's first painting of New York was sold the first afternoon it was on display. "No one ever objected to my painting New York after that," she recalled. She continued painting the city until about 1929.

Chapter 5

Bleached Bones and Desert Dust

In 1929, the Museum of Modern Art in New York included five of O'Keeffe's works in a special exhibit, *Paintings by Nineteen Living Americans.* This was a great honor.

By this time, O'Keeffe was tired of summers at Lake George. Stieglitz's family and friends were always there. She needed time alone to work and new subjects to paint. She spent that summer painting in New Mexico and the Southwest. After that, she went back there again and again to live and paint. She painted

O'Keeffe began spending her summers at Ghost Ranch in New Mexico. She bought the ranch in 1940 and lived there on and off for the rest of her life.

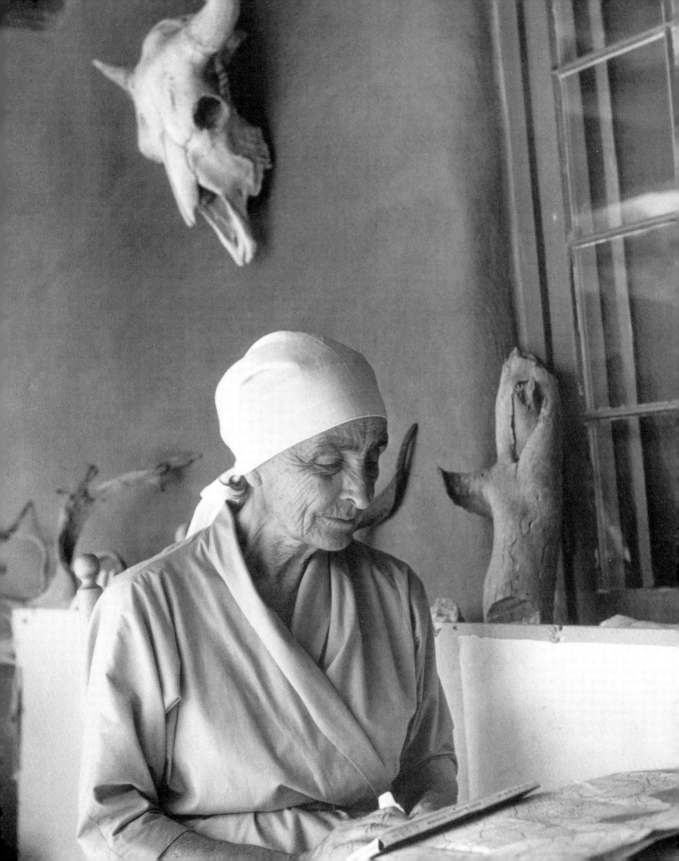

White Flower on Red Earth, #1 (1943). Even many years after her "flower phase" was over, O'Keeffe would return to the subject.

the hills and the churches. She painted the bleached bones of the desert. She painted skulls floating over mountains.

It was a big change in her life. Stieglitz did not like to travel. His life and work was in New York City and Lake George. He loved his wife very much, and he missed her when she was gone. But he stayed behind.

O'Keeffe returned to New York each fall to spend the winters with Stieglitz and her New York friends. In 1936, O'Keeffe and Stieglitz moved to a penthouse apartment on East Fifty-fourth Street in New York. But O'Keeffe's heart was in New Mexico.

The next summer, she stayed at a place called Ghost Ranch in New Mexico. The house felt like home to O'Keeffe. A few years later, she bought it.

She became fascinated with the animal bones she found everywhere around Ghost Ranch. She painted lots of skulls and other types of bones. She liked showing bones in new and unusual ways.

In 1945 and 1946, two important retrospective exhibits of her work took place—one at the Chicago Institute of Art, and the other at the Museum of Modern Art in New York. O'Keeffe had become an important artist.

One day in July 1946, O'Keeffe received a telegram. Her eighty-two-year-old husband had suffered a stroke. She immediately flew to New York. She stayed by Stieglitz's side in the hospital and was there when he died.

Chapter 6

Lone Artist at Abiquiu

O'Keeffe remained in New York for many months to take care of Stieglitz's photographs and paintings. Then she returned to New Mexico in 1949 for good.

She had bought a second house there a few years earlier. This one was a ruin near an old town called Abiquiu. As soon as she had seen it, she had fallen in love with it. The patio and the patio door fascinated her. She painted them many times. For the rest of her life she would

When O'Keeffe first saw the house at Abiquiu, she found a door in the wall around the patio. "That wall with a door in it was something I had to have," she later wrote.

spend spring and summer every year at Abiquiu. In fall and winter, she would live in her house at Ghost Ranch.

As always, she loved to be alone. That was when she did her best work.

O'Keeffe always remembered the advice of William Merritt Chase to be "artistic in every way." She had become a kind of celebrity—someone who was famous and admired and in the news

often. In her later years, she always dressed in black for photographs and visitors. She took great care to present herself as someone special.

O'Keeffe received many awards and honors in the 1970s and 1980s. In 1971, she received the Gold Medal for Painting from the National Institute of Arts and Letters. In 1977, United States President Gerald Ford presented her with the Presidential Medal of Freedom, the highest civilian honor. In 1970, the Whitney Museum of American Art held a major retrospective exhibition of O'Keeffe's work. The exhibit also toured Chicago and San Francisco. It was very popular.

Near Abiquiu, New Mexico (1941). Ghost Ranch was in the middle of nowhere. It was far from everything, and that's what O'Keeffe liked about it. The nearest town was a tiny village called Abiquiu seventeen miles away. O'Keeffe loved to paint the light and space of the desert.

Chapter 7

Fading Light

Then, at the peak of her fame, O'Keeffe got some terrible news: She was losing her eyesight. The central part of her vision was becoming blurred. Soon, she was almost completely blind. She could no longer see lines and shapes and colors. She could no longer paint.

That year, she found a new secretary and friend, Virginia Robertson. They began working on a book titled *Georgia O'Keeffe*. It was about O'Keeffe's life and work. It described how she felt about her paintings. Georgia talked on tape about her memories and thoughts. Virginia listened and typed her words on paper.

Before it was finished, though, Robertson left. At about this time, a young man stopped by O'Keeffe's gate at Ghost Ranch. Many young artists came to visit her. They admired the dedication she had to her work. They wanted to learn from her.

This visitor was working at Ghost Ranch. His name was John Hamilton, but everyone called him Juan. He had brown eyes and a big mustache that reminded Georgia of Stieglitz. O'Keeffe found that Hamilton was well educated. He helped her finish her book. It was published in 1976 and became a bestseller.

Hamilton shared many interests with O'Keeffe. He made pottery, and she encouraged him. He gave her an arm to lean on when she walked in the hills. She liked his sense of humor. He was her secretary and very close friend in the last years of her life.

Over the next ten years, they traveled and worked together. Hamilton showed O'Keeffe how to make pottery. She said she liked to try to "make the clay speak." She didn't need her eyes for this art. She could feel the smoothness and shape of the clay with her hands.

In 1984, O'Keeffe became ill and moved from her home at Abiquiu to Santa Fe. She died at Saint Vincent's Hospital in Santa Fe on March 6, 1986. She was ninety-eight years old.

The Georgia O'Keeffe Museum opened in Santa Fe, New Mexico, in July 1997. It is the only museum in the United States that is devoted primarily to the work of a major woman artist.

During her long and productive life, O'Keeffe gave the world two thousand paintings, drawings, and sculptures. Today, she is remembered as a

The Georgia O'Keeffe Museum opened in Santa Fe, New Mexico, in 1997. O'Keeffe loved New Mexico to the end. According to her wishes, after O'Keeffe's death, Juan Hamilton scattered her ashes in New Mexico.

great artist. She was also an amazing woman. Perhaps most of all, people think of O'Keeffe as a rare human being—one who knew who she was. And who was always true to herself.

Timeline

1887   Born November 15 in Sun Prairie, Wisconsin.

1901   Enters Sacred Heart Academy in Madison, Wisconsin.

1902   O'Keeffe family moves to Williamsburg, Virginia.

1903–1905   Finishes high school at Chatham Episcopal Institute in Virginia.

1907   Studies at the Art Students League in New York City.

1908   Makes first visit to Alfred Stieglitz's 291 gallery in New York.

1908–1910   Stops painting. Works as a commercial artist in Chicago.

1916   Stieglitz exhibits O'Keeffe's drawings at the 291 gallery in New York.

1917   First solo exhibition opens, at 291 gallery in New York.

Timeline

1923 Stieglitz opens the first annual exhibition of O'Keeffe's work.

1924 Marries Alfred Stieglitz. Begins painting large flowers.

1925 Moves with Stieglitz to New York. Begins cityscapes.

1937 Stays for the first time in house she later buys at Ghost Ranch, New Mexico.

1945 Purchases property near the ancient town of Abiquiu, New Mexico.

1946 Stieglitz dies at age eighty-two.

1949 Moves permanently to New Mexico.

1976 The book *Georgia O'Keeffe* is published and becomes a bestseller.

1977 Receives the Presidential Medal of Freedom, the highest American civilian honor.

1986 Dies March 6 at a hospital in Santa Fe at age ninety-eight.

Words to Know

art critics — People who are considered experts in art, who judge art, write about it, and have a say in how valuable it is.

canvas — Type of heavy cloth, stretched over a frame, on which artists paint pictures.

commercial art — Drawings, paintings, and other artwork created to promote a business—for example, advertisements.

modernists — Group of artists who painted in new ways; they often painted non-realistic shapes, objects, or scenes.

on exhibit — On display for people to see. Museums put artists' work on exhibit.

retrospective exhibition — Art show that displays an artist's past work, in honor of a long and successful career.

Georgia O'Keeffe

Internet Addresses

The best way to learn more about any artist, including Georgia O'Keeffe, is to see the art—the real thing, not just photographs of it. That is easy if you happen to live in a large city with a large art museum, such as New York or Santa Fe. But if you do not, try the Internet. The Web sites for O'Keeffe listed on the next page were written for people of all ages, so the text may be a bit too hard for you to get through. That is okay, though—you are just visiting for the pictures.

The Georgia O'Keeffe Museum is the only museum in the United States devoted to a major female artist. It houses the largest collection of O'Keeffe's works in the world.
http://www.okeeffemuseum.org

Artcyclopedia, The Fine Art Search Engine: Georgia O'Keeffe. Nearly 100 links to O'Keeffe's paintings online, as well as books and articles about her and her work.
http://www.artcyclopedia.com/artists/okeeffe_georgia.html

Index